WONDER WOMAN™ MYTHOLOGY

Wonder Woman and the World of Myth

by STEVE KORTÉ

Wonder Woman created by William Moulton Marston

Consultant:
Laurel Bowman
Department of Greek and Roman Studies
University of Victoria
British Columbia, Canada

CAPSTONE PRESS
a capstone imprint

Published by Capstone Press in 2017
1710 Roe Crest Drive
North Mankato, Minnesota 56003
www.mycapstone.com

Library of Congress Cataloging-in-Publication Data is available on
the Library of Congress website.

ISBN: 978-1-5157-4582-2 (library binding)
ISBN: 978-1-5157-4595-2 (eBook PDF)

Summary: Introduces a variety of places, objects, and creatures from
Greek, Roman, Norse, and other world mythologies, and explores
how they are woven into the fabric of Wonder Woman's backstory.

Editor: Christopher Harbo

Designer: Tracy McCabe

Creative Director: Bob Lentz

Production Specialist: Katy LaVigne

Image Credits:
Capstone: Eduardo Garcia, 19, McLean Kendree, 23, Scott
Altman, 9, 11, 15, 17, 21, 25; iStockphoto: Sergiy Pomogayev, 27;
Shutterstock: Alexandra Petruk, 6, CP DC Press, 9 (inset), Elena
Schweitzer, cover, (right), Felix Lipov, 27, (inset), Juan Manuel
Rodriguez, cover, (bottom), Kisialiou Yury, 14, Lena_graphics,
cover, (left), 29, Mila Atkovska, 16, S-F, 11 (inset), Sin314, 28, Vuk
Kostic, 13, Warner Brothers, 17 (Aquaman), throughout (Wonder
Woman and backgrounds)

Printed and bound in the USA.
010061S17

TABLE OF CONTENTS

A World of Myth

Myths are stories that explain the origins of the world and how humans came to exist. Although ancient myths may seem strange or wild to us today, the people who first told them really believed that they were true. As the myths were handed down from one **generation** to another, they became some of the most popular and powerful stories ever told.

The stories of Wonder Woman are filled with mythological monsters, villains, gods, and goddesses. From Ares to Zeus, the Amazon princess has fought against and with a staggering number of mythological characters. Along with these characters, their other-worldly **artifacts** and their fantastic lands have all made appearances in her legendary tales as well.

Now you can enter the world of mythology in a whole new way. Not only will you learn about the most remarkable characters, places, and artifacts of classic mythology. You will also discover how they have defined the life of one of the world's most powerful super heroes: Wonder Woman!

FACT
Wonder Woman's comic book history dates back more than 75 years. She made her first appearance in *All-Star Comics* #8 in December 1941.

generation—a group of people born around the same time

artifact—an object made or changed by human beings, especially a tool or weapon used in the past

CHAPTER 1

Warrior Women

AMAZONS

The Amazons were a tribe of fierce warrior women in Greek mythology. It was believed that the Amazons were **descended** from the war god Ares. They had their own laws and government. They also spent most of their time hunting or training for combat. Most important of all, the Amazons did not want to be ruled or controlled by men. Although they did have male servants to perform small tasks for them, the Amazons didn't usually seek out the company of men.

THE AMAZON RIVER

The 16th century Spanish explorer Francisco de Orellana gave the Amazon River its name. He claimed to have seen tall fighting women while exploring the South American jungle. He named the river after the Amazons of Greek mythology.

In the mythology of Wonder Woman, the Amazons broke into two groups after a battle destroyed their home. The warrior queen Antiope headed one group. They moved to Egypt and became known as the Bana-Mighdall tribe of Amazons. Queen Hippolyta ruled the other group. They lived together peacefully on a remote island and were granted **immortality** by the goddesses. Thousands of years later, Hippolyta sculpted a child out of clay and asked the goddesses to bring it to life. This first child born to the Amazons was named Diana. She would later become Wonder Woman.

descend—to belong to a later generation of the same family

immortality—the ability to live forever

CONTESTS

Contests play an important role in many tales of Greek mythology. In fact, today's Olympic Games are based on festivals held from 776 BC to AD 393 in Olympia, Greece, to honor the gods. One example of contests in myth involves a Greek princess named Atalanta. She was left on a mountaintop to die by her father. Raised in the wilderness, she developed incredible hunting and athletic skills. Most importantly, she became famous for a series of athletic contests in which she defeated every man who **proposed** to her. She won wrestling matches against the strongest male champions. She used her spears and arrows to defeat other men in hunting games.

Princess Diana became Wonder Woman after she participated in an important athletic contest on her hidden home island of Themyscira. It happened after the Amazons discovered that the war god Ares was threatening humankind. Queen Hippolyta called for a contest to choose one Amazon champion to travel to the human world to defeat Ares. Diana was **forbidden** to take part, but she disguised herself and easily defeated the other participants. Hippolyta had no choice but to declare her daughter the winner.

propose—to ask someone to marry you
forbidden—not permitted or allowed

ATALANTA

FACT
The first modern Olympic Games were held in Athens, Greece, in 1896. Today they draw athletes from around the world to compete in both summer and winter sports.

CHAPTER 2

Amazing Realms

MOUNT OLYMPUS

The powerful gods and goddesses of Greek mythology lived high on Mount Olympus, where they had a wonderful view of all of Greece. Ancient Greeks believed that Olympus was the highest mountain in the world. In the myths, Olympus had many peaks, and each one was the home of a different god. Zeus, the ruler of all the gods, lived on the highest peak. In some myths, Mount Olympus was part of heaven and not attached to Earth at all.

Life on Mount Olympus was occasionally peaceful, with its residents resting and feasting. More often, though, the gods and goddesses spent their time arguing, playing tricks on each other, or plotting **revenge**. Though they were immortal, the gods and goddesses experienced the same emotions as their **mortal** subjects. Unlike mortals, though, the gods caused earthquakes and other disasters when they grew angry.

In the tales of Wonder Woman, Mount Olympus was destroyed by Darkseid, an evil god who hated all of Earth's heroes. A new home for the gods was created by Zeus, Hades, and Poseidon. Called New Olympus, it was a magical kingdom that floated above Earth in another dimension. For a short time, Princess Diana served as the goddess of truth and lived on Mount Olympus. She ultimately decided to return to her role as Wonder Woman.

revenge—an action taken to repay harm done

mortal—human, referring to a being who will eventually die

FACT
The real Mount Olympus is the highest mountain in Greece. It rises almost 10,000 feet (3,048 meters) above sea level.

HADES

After the Greek god Zeus defeated his father, he became the ruler of the gods. He then divided the universe into three parts. Zeus claimed heaven for himself, and he gave the seas to his brother Poseidon. His other brother, Hades, ruled the underworld of dead souls. Eventually, that realm would also come to be known as Hades.

All dead souls — good, in-between, and bad — traveled to Hades. To reach the underworld, the dead took a ferry across the River Styx. Three paths then led to their ultimate homes. Good souls traveled to the Elysian Fields, where they found blue skies, music, and feasting. Souls that were neither good nor bad took the middle path to the Meadows of Asphodel. There they wandered forever in the mist. Evil souls took the third path down to the pits of Tartarus. There they were forced to **endure** horrible punishments forever.

Princess Diana first journeyed into Hades during an Amazon contest. Queen Hippolyta tossed an apple into the depths of Hades to see if Diana could catch it before it hit the ground. Cerberus, the giant guard dog at the gates of Hades, quickly caught the apple in its mouth. Before he could drop it on the ground, Wonder Woman forcefully drew in her breath. The apple flew from the dog's mouth and into her hands. Years later, Diana rescued both the god Hermes and the Amazon warrior Artemis from Hades.

FACT
The three-headed dog Cerberus fiercely guarded the entrance to Hades. His mouths dripped deadly saliva, and his necks were surrounded by **venomous** snakes.

endure—to put up with something unpleasant or painful

venomous—having or producing a poison called venom

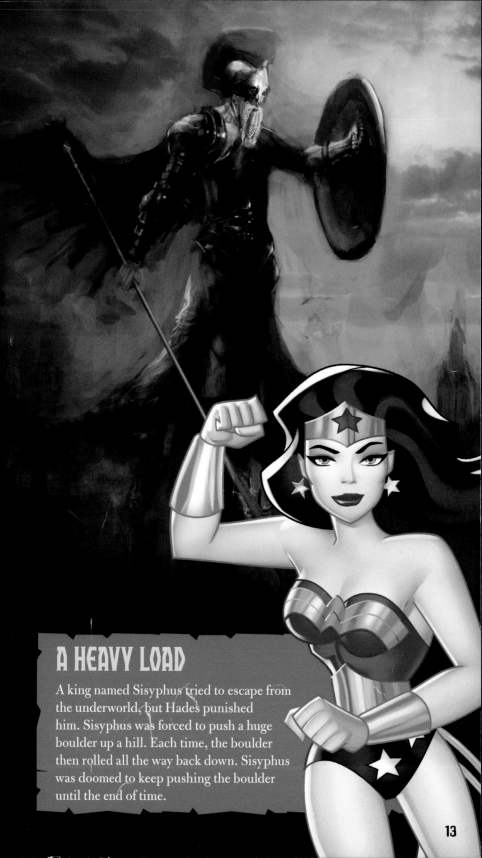

A HEAVY LOAD

A king named Sisyphus tried to escape from
the underworld, but Hades punished
him. Sisyphus was forced to push a huge
boulder up a hill. Each time, the boulder
then rolled all the way back down. Sisyphus
was doomed to keep pushing the boulder
until the end of time.

13

THEMISCYRA

Greek myths vary on the location of the home of the Amazons. Some stories placed it in northeastern Greece, near the Aegean Sea. Others said that it was Themiscyra, in Turkey. Still others placed it in Libya, or even southern Russia. Regardless of the location, the Amazons lived by hunting — but not everything they captured was an animal. One story tells how the Amazons who settled by the Aegean Sea lured sailors to their shores. After they welcomed them to their homeland, they kidnapped them to use as slaves!

In the tales of Wonder Woman, the Amazons lived in the Greek city of Themyscira. After Hercules and his army destroyed the city, Queen Hippolyta led half of the Amazons to a faraway tropical island that was hidden from the rest of the world. They called their new island home Themyscira as well. It was so beautiful that some called it Paradise Island. Diana became the first child to be born on Themyscira 3,000 years later. She was also the island's first princess.

FACT

In Wonder Woman **lore**, the island of Themyscira is hidden in the center of the Bermuda Triangle. This area east of Florida in the Atlantic Ocean is famous for mysterious disappearances of ships and aircraft.

lore—a collection of knowledge and traditions of a particular group that has been passed down over generations

FACT

In Greek myth, the Amazons' home is spelled "Themiscyra." In Wonder Woman lore, it is "Themyscira."

ATLANTIS

There are many myths about the legendary lost realm of Atlantis that was located at the bottom of the Atlantic Ocean. The Greek philosopher Plato wrote that Atlantis was a wealthy island kingdom that was founded by the god Poseidon. When its residents became too greedy, Poseidon destroyed Atlantis with tidal waves and an earthquake. It then sank to the ocean floor. More recent myths have **speculated** that Atlantis was the home of aliens from outer space who chose to establish their base deep within the ocean.

In the tales of Wonder Woman, Atlantis sank to the bottom of the ocean thousands of years ago. Miraculously, the city's scientists supplied a **serum** that allowed the citizens of Atlantis to breathe underwater. Wonder Woman often worked alongside the hero Aquaman to protect the people of Atlantis.

When a space alien known as Imperiex declared war on Earth, Aquaman saved Atlantis from destruction by sending it 3,000 years into the past. Just as its citizens were about to become slaves to ancient super-beings, Wonder Woman and the Justice League's team of heroes traveled through time to rescue the people of Atlantis.

FACT
Atlantis may have been based on the real Greek island of Thera, known today as Santorini. It was destroyed in a volcanic eruption thousands of years ago.

speculate—to think about or discuss what is uncertain or unknown

serum—a liquid used to prevent or cure a disease

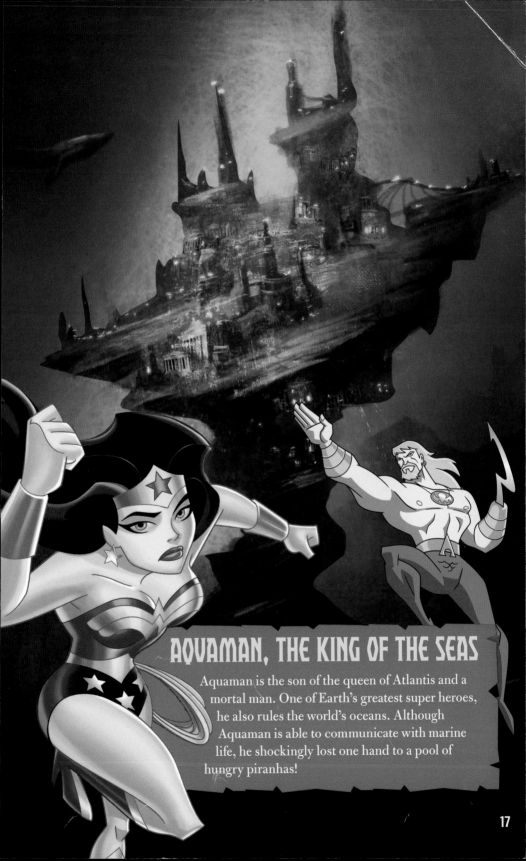

AQUAMAN, THE KING OF THE SEAS

Aquaman is the son of the queen of Atlantis and a mortal man. One of Earth's greatest super heroes, he also rules the world's oceans. Although Aquaman is able to communicate with marine life, he shockingly lost one hand to a pool of hungry piranhas!

VALHALLA

The Vikings had great respect for their gods, especially the all-powerful Odin. In the tales of Norse mythology, Odin was in charge of a legendary and beautiful hall where dead soldiers gathered. It was called Valhalla. This giant building had 640 doors and room for 800 dead warriors. The Vikings believed that these brave soldiers would stay in Valhalla and wait for the end of the world. That end time was called Ragnarök. When Ragnarök arrived, a beautiful new world would emerge.

Wonder Woman's most dramatic encounter with the Norse gods occurred when she and Superman traveled to Valhalla. Thor, the son of Odin, asked them to help defend the mighty hall from an army of demons known as the Vrgtsmyth. The heroes were magically trapped within Valhalla for a battle that lasted 1,000 years. In the end, Wonder Woman and Superman defeated the demons. Thor then returned the two heroes to present-day Earth.

ODIN

THOR

FEARLESS FIGHTERS

Several armies helped the Norse gods. The Valkyries were
skilled female fighters. The Berserkers were savage warriors
that wore bearskins and never felt any pain. And the Einherjar
were dead soldiers that rose again to fight for the gods.

CHAPTER 3

Incredible Items

THE GOLDEN BELT

The Greek goddess Hera hated the hero Hercules. She caused him to lose his mind and murder his own children. He was then sentenced to perform 12 difficult tasks, known as labors. One of the tasks was to obtain the golden belt worn by Queen Hippolyta. It had been a gift from her father to show that she was the mightiest Amazon warrior. In one version of the myth, Hippolyta agreed to give the belt to Hercules. In another myth, Hercules killed her and stole the belt.

In Wonder Woman's mythology, the goddess Gaea was the grandmother of the Olympian gods and the powerful protector of Earth. The two queens of the Amazons, Hippolyta and Antiope, were each given shining gold belts that were known as the Golden Girdles of Gaea. Each belt had magical powers to protect its wearer. Many years after Hercules stole Hippolyta's belt, it was **transformed** by the goddess Hestia into Wonder Woman's magical Lasso of Truth.

transform—change a great deal, such as in your actions or appearance

HIPPOLYTA

AMAZING BRACELETS

In addition to her golden belt, Diana also received two bracelets that were made from pieces of Zeus' shield. The bracelets were almost indestructible. Even bullets would bounce off them.

PANDORA'S BOX

In Greek mythology, Pandora was the first mortal woman. The mighty god Zeus commanded Hephaestus and other gods to create her from clay and water. Then all of the gods gave her gifts. One gift was the item known as Pandora's Box, and there are several different tales about it.

In one story, the gods gave Pandora a sealed jar and told her never to open it. When she disobeyed their order and removed the lid, all of the **plagues** of humankind escaped from the jar. Pain, sadness, jealousy, and disease spread throughout the world of mortals.

In another version of the story, the jar was filled with only good items, including blessings, kindness, and hope. When Pandora opened the jar, most of the items escaped and flew back to Mount Olympus. The one item that remained was hope. Mortal men and women were doomed to suffer through life with only hope to bring them comfort.

On Wonder Woman's home island of Themyscira, two Amazons always stood guard outside a giant door known as Doom's Doorway. The world's most dangerous mythological monsters were chained within dungeons far below that door. The evils of Pandora's Box were also safely locked behind Doom's Doorway.

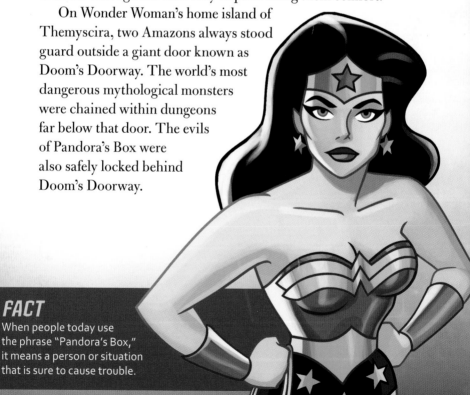

FACT
When people today use the phrase "Pandora's Box," it means a person or situation that is sure to cause trouble.

plague—a very serious disease that spreads quickly to
many people and often causes death

APPLE OF DISCORD

Eris was the Greek goddess of conflict, and she was so troublesome that Zeus **banished** her from Mount Olympus. One time, Zeus was planning a wedding for two of his favorite subjects. He invited all of the other gods and goddesses to the wedding, but he did not invite Eris. He knew that she would ruin the event.

Eris was furious when she found out, and she showed up at the wedding feast. She carried a golden apple, on which she had written "for the fairest." Eris then threw the apple into the crowd. All of the goddesses rushed forward to claim the apple, and soon a terrible battle broke out between Aphrodite, Athena, and Hera. Each one wanted to prove that she was the fairest. The fight between the goddesses continued for days and weeks after that. Ultimately, it led to the start of the Trojan War.

banish—to send away forever

ERIS

In Wonder Woman's world, Eris had an entire tree of apples that was located in the pits of Tartarus. Anyone who ate one of her apples was filled with anger and hatred. Even the tree itself was dangerous. Victims caught within the tree's moving vines would magically be turned into wood. Wonder Woman threw her Golden Lasso of Truth around the tree, which caused the tree to burst into flames. The tree and all of its apples crumbled into ashes.

SANDALS OF HERMES

Hermes was the fastest Greek god of them all. He wore a pair of sandals with tiny wings on them. They gave him the power to run from Mount Olympus to the world of mortals and then to the depths of Hades. Hermes ran so fast that he was sometimes a blur! Some claimed that his sandals allowed Hermes to fly. In one myth, the hero Perseus was determined to kill the monstrous Medusa. Hermes loaned his sandals to Perseus in order to help him on his quest.

In the myths of Wonder Woman, Hermes gave a pair of his winged sandals to Princess Diana so that she could travel quickly from Themyscira to Man's World. The sandals did more than allow her to run fast. Because they responded to the desires of the person who was wearing them, the sandals gave Diana the power of flight.

FACT
When Hermes was a baby, he ran from his cradle to play a trick on Apollo. He hid Apollo's herd of cattle!

FACT
In Roman mythology, Hermes was known as Mercury.

CHAPTER 4
Crude Creatures

CENTAURS

Not all creatures of myth were monsters. In Greek mythology, centaurs were half-man and half-horse, half-tame and half-wild. Although only a few centaurs were truly evil, most of them had very bad manners. One time, a herd of centaurs attended the royal wedding of King Pirithous, the ruler of Thessaly. The centaurs became rowdy, drinking all the punch and eating all the food. Even worse, they started fighting with the human guests and kicked them with their hooves. A few humans even died! After that, the king banished all centaurs from Thessaly.

In Greek mythology, and in the world of Wonder Woman, there was one wise centaur. His name was Chiron, and he was much gentler than his rude relatives. Some claimed that Chiron was a half-brother to Zeus and not even related to other centaurs. The centaur Chiron became a teacher to Wonder Woman and helped her to develop her hunting and archery skills. Years later, Chiron even performed surgery on Wonder Woman and saved her life after she was injured in battle.

FACT
Chiron the centaur inspired the Centaurus **constellation**. Alpha Centauri, its brightest star, is the closest star to our sun.

constellation—a group of stars that forms a shape

acclaim—praise

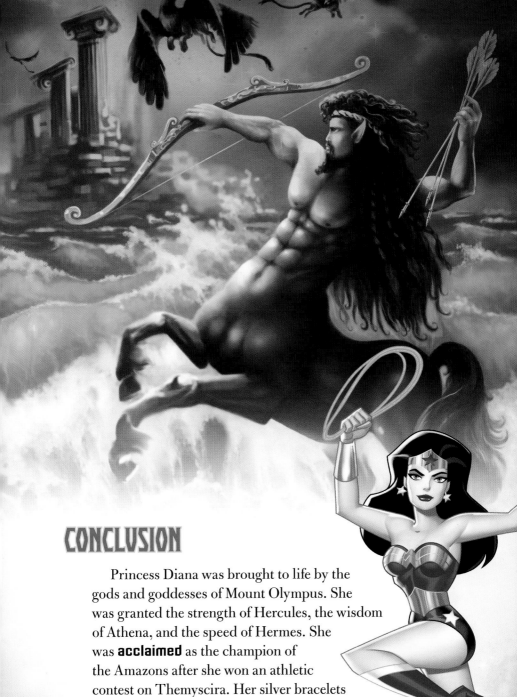

CONCLUSION

Princess Diana was brought to life by the gods and goddesses of Mount Olympus. She was granted the strength of Hercules, the wisdom of Athena, and the speed of Hermes. She was **acclaimed** as the champion of the Amazons after she won an athletic contest on Themyscira. Her silver bracelets and Golden Lasso of Truth gave her great powers. The legendary tales of Wonder Woman may thrill us. But they also allow us to learn more about the incredible places, artifacts, and characters from the world of mythology.

GLOSSARY

acclaim (uh-KLAYM)—praise

artifact (AHR-tuh-fakt)—an object made or changed by human beings, especially a tool or weapon used in the past

banish (BAN-ish)—to send away forever

constellation (kahn-stuh-LAY-shuhn)—a group of stars that forms a shape

descend (dee-SEND)—to belong to a later generation of the same family

endure (en-DUR)—to put up with something unpleasant or painful

forbidden (fur-BID-uhn)—not permitted or allowed

generation (jen-uh-RAY-shuhn)—a group of people born around the same time

immortality (i-mor-TAL-uh-tee)—the ability to live forever

lore (LORE)—a collection of knowledge and traditions of a particular group that has been passed down over generations

mortal (MOR-tuhl)—human, referring to a being who will eventually die

plague (PAYG)—a very serious disease that spreads quickly to many people and often causes death

propose (pruh-POZE)—to ask someone to marry you

revenge (rih-VENJ)—an action taken to repay harm done

serum (SIHR-uhm)—a liquid used to prevent or cure a disease

speculate (SPEK-yuh-late)—to think about or discuss what is uncertain or unknown

transform (trans-FORM)—change a great deal, such as in your actions or appearance

venomous (VEN-uhm-us)—having or producing a poison called venom

READ MORE

Dickman, Nancy. *Ancient Greece.* History Hunters. North Mankato, Minn.: Capstone Press, 2017.

Ferrell, David. *Achilles and the Trojan War: Jr. Graphic Myths.* Greek Heros. New York: PowerKids Press, 2014.

Griffin, Ingrid. *The Story of Hercules.* Stories in the Stars. New York: Gareth Stevens Publishing, 2016.

Weakland, Mark. *The Adventures of Perseus: A Graphic Retelling.* Ancient Myths. North Mankato, Minn.: Capstone Press, 2015.

INTERNET SITES

FactHound offers a safe, fun way to find Internet sites related to this book. All of the sites on FactHound have been researched by our staff.

Here's all you do:

Visit *www.facthound.com*

Type in this code: 9781515745822

Check out projects, games and lots more at
www.capstonekids.com

INDEX